Guitar Soloing:

FROM**PENTATONIC** **SCALES**TO**MODES**

Use Major & Minor Pentatonic Scales to Play Exciting Modal Solos

JOSEPH**ALEXANDER**

FUNDAMENTAL**CHANGES**

Guitar Soloing: From Pentatonic Scales to Modes

Use Major & Minor Pentatonic Scales to Play Exciting Modal Solos

ISBN: 978-1-78933-401-2

Published by **www.fundamental-changes.com**

Copyright © 2023 Joseph Alexander

Edited by Tim Pettingale

www.fundamental-changes.com

Instagram: **FundamentalChanges**

For over 350 Free Guitar Lessons with Videos Check Out

www.fundamental-changes.com

With huge thanks yet again to the incredible Levi Clay for making this book happen.

Check out his Patreon and become a master transcriber.

Cover Image Copyright: Shutterstock, Boonchuay1970

Contents

About the Author

Joseph Alexander is one of the most prolific writers of modern guitar tuition methods.

He has sold over 1,000,000 books that have educated and inspired a generation of upcoming musicians. His uncomplicated tuition style is based around breaking down the barriers between theory and performance and making music accessible to all.

Educated at London's Guitar Institute and Leeds College of Music, where he earned a degree in Jazz Studies, Joseph has taught thousands of students and written over 50 books on playing the guitar.

He is the managing director of *Fundamental Changes Ltd.*, a publishing company whose sole purpose is to create the highest quality music tuition books and pay excellent royalties to writers and musicians.

Fundamental Changes has published over 200 music tuition books and is currently accepting submissions from prospective authors and teachers of all instruments.

Get in touch via **customercontact@fundamental-changes.com** if you'd like to work with us on a project.

Once again, I find myself in huge debt to the incredible Levi Clay for making this book happen.

Check out his Patreon and become a master transcriber.

Introduction

For guitar players who are starting to solo, a common question is how to use *modes* in their playing.

Often, they think there is some big secret that only a select handful of guitarists know, and that they need to be indoctrinated into some sort of shrouded cult to discover the true art of improvisation. Despite that sounding like quite a cool club to be a part of, the truth is sadly a lot simpler.

- A mode is any seven-note scale

- There are seven common modes (two of which you probably won't use very much)

- Each of these modes creates a different musical mood

- That's it!

Of course, there's a bit of theory to learn about where they come from, how to form them, and when to use them… and we'll cover all that in detail later. But for now, all you need to know is that modes are scales that have different characteristics and create different musical moods.

If you're reading this book, I assume you've already explored some minor pentatonic soloing and maybe played a bit of blues or classic rock. The minor pentatonic sound is at the heart of both of those styles and is the most vocal, important, and idiomatic part of the guitar's language to master. However, often when guitarists come to learn modes, they suddenly treat them as a completely separate world (and language) to pentatonic soloing. This can often result in their soloing sounding quite unmusical and somehow "forced".

This book is designed to take you smoothly and *musically* from the world of minor pentatonic playing into the world of modal soloing. You'll get "inside" the modes and learn to see them from a pentatonic viewpoint.

The whole approach is based around a very simple idea.

Every seven-note mode is built around a five-note pentatonic scale that you already know. All you need to do is add *two notes* to the pentatonic scale to create the mode and introduce a whole new world of soloing opportunities.

For example, compare the A Minor Pentatonic scale on the left to the A Dorian mode on the right. I've highlighted the two new notes for you.

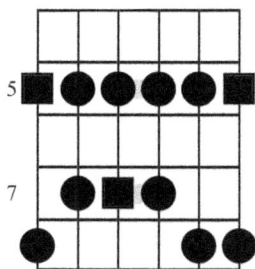

A Minor Pentatonic
Shape 1

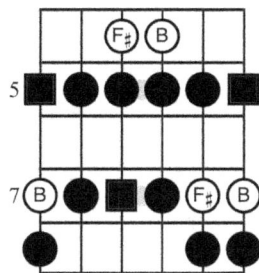

A Dorian
Shape 1

As you can see, there is a huge amount in common between the minor pentatonic scale and Dorian mode, and that learning Dorian as a minor pentatonic with two added notes has a wide range of advantages.

First, it'll help you see, *hear,* and understand how modes relate to the pentatonic language you already know. This will help you avoid the common trap of learning modes as new, daunting entities that sit independently of your current knowledge and require a whole new language and approach to use.

Second, when you see modes like this, all the musical pentatonic nuances you already use (such as bends, slides and vibrato) *automatically* get carried into the unique characteristics of each mode. This enables you to immediately play modes *musically* and avoid the awkward gear changes that often occur when switching from pentatonic to modal playing.

Lastly, when you do want to transition from "classic" pentatonic vocabulary into more modern modal playing, that transition becomes smooth and musical instead of a rigid "here are my pentatonic licks, now here are my modal licks" approach.

The best thing about learning your modes around pentatonic shapes is that it's easy, fun and, above all, immediate! By just adding a couple of extra notes to a pentatonic scale you'll unlock a whole new dimension of musical expression.

If you're ready to get started, grab your guitar and let's dive in!

Have fun!

Joseph

Get the Audio

The audio files for this book are available to download for free from **www.fundamental-changes.com.** The link is in the top right-hand corner. Click on the "Guitar" link then simply select this book title from the drop-down menu and follow the instructions to get the audio.

We recommend that you download the files directly to your computer, not to your tablet, and extract them there before adding them to your media library. You can then put them onto your tablet, or smart phone. On the download page there are instructions, and we also provide technical support via the contact form.

For over 350 free guitar lessons with videos check out:

www.fundamental-changes.com

Join our free Facebook Community of Cool Musicians

www.facebook.com/groups/fundamentalguitar

Tag us for a share on Instagram: **FundamentalChanges**

Chapter One: Minor Pentatonics and Theory Recap

Before we dive into our exploration of modes, it's important that you have a grasp of the five common minor pentatonic scale shapes. While a lot of our study will be based around the first and most common shape of the scale, for you to expand this concept all over the neck you'll eventually need to know all five positions.

In this book we'll be working in the key of A and it is essential that you know the first shape of the A Minor Pentatonic scale shown below.

A Minor Pentatonic
Shape 1

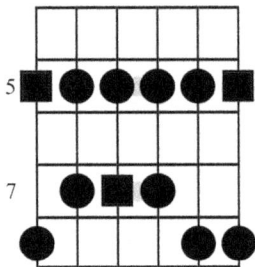

Example 1a:

There are five common shapes for the minor pentatonic scale and the other four are shown in the examples below. If you're not certain of these shapes, treat this section as a parallel learning task as you work through the book.

These shapes are important to know, and as soon as you can play them, you'll have access to the entire range of the fretboard which will allow you to play your new vocabulary all over the neck.

It's important that you know they all contain the same five notes (A C D E and G) and simply map out these notes across the fretboard.

A Minor Pentatonic
Shape 2

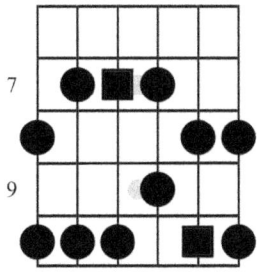

Example 1b:

```
T  |                    8--10    8                                        |
A  |        7--9    8--10          10--8                                  |
B  |  7--10             9--7                                7--10         |
   |                         10--7                  7                 7   |
   |                                    10     10--8--10               |
```

A Minor Pentatonic
Shape 3

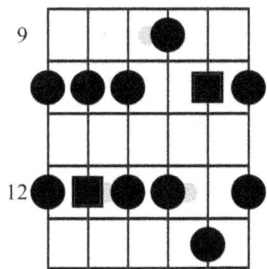

Example 1c:

```
T  |                    10--13   10    12--10                            |
A  |        9--12    10--13          13--10                              |
B  |  12--10--12             12--9                         10--12        |
   |                              12--10           12--10          10--12|
   |                                        12--10--12                   |
```

A Minor Pentatonic
Shape 4

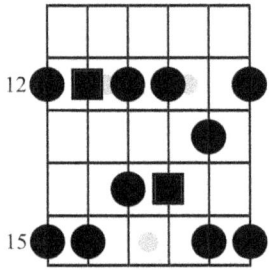

Example 1d:

A Minor Pentatonic
Shape 5

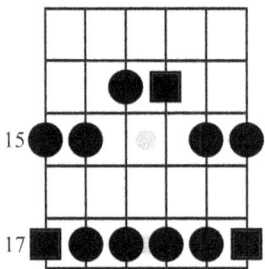

Example 1e:

I won't dwell too much on the pentatonic shapes, because if you're reading this book, I assume you have a good portion of this knowledge down. However, in the following examples I want to give you three exercises to help you understand how the shapes link together.

The first exercise starts on the bottom note of A Minor Pentatonic shape one, then ascends each shape in turn up to move up the fretboard all the way to shape five.

Example 1f:

The next exercise begins from the lowest note of shape one and ascends the scale before sliding up into the highest note of shape two. The cxercise continues by descending all the way through shape two before sliding up into the lowest note of shape three. Ascend through shape three and repeat the process all the way up to where shape one occurs again at the top of the fretboard.

Example 1g:

The final exercise reverses the previous idea and repeats the process from the top of shape five all the way down to the bottom of shape one at the 5th fret.

Example 1h:

These exercises were a brief recap of the pentatonic scale positions. While they're not essential study to use this book, you will get a lot more out from it if you understand how the five shapes fit together.

For more information, I do suggest you check out my books,

Minor Pentatonic Soloing Connections

And

The CAGED System and 100 Licks for Blues Guitar

Getting Started: A Brief Introduction to Modes

Any scale can be described by a *formula*, kind of like algebra for music. Don't worry, before you zone out, I promise this is really easy!

The most basic scale in music is the major scale. In the key of C it contains the notes C D E F G A B.

The characteristic sound of the major scale is created by the unique pattern of steps and half-steps (tones and semitones) between those notes.

The distance between C and D is a whole step / one tone (two frets on the fretboard)

The distance between D and E is a whole step / one tone (two frets on the fretboard)

The distance between E and F is a *half step* / one semitone (one fret on the fretboard)

The distance between F and G is a whole step / one tone (two frets on the fretboard)

The distance between G and A is a whole step / one tone (two frets on the fretboard)

The distance between A and B is a whole step / one tone (two frets on the fretboard)

The distance between B and C is a *half step* / one semitone (one fret on the fretboard)

This means that the pattern of tones and semitones in the major scale from the root note goes as follows:

Tone, Tone, Semitone, Tone, Tone, Tone, Semitone.

(or Step, Step, Half-step, Step, Step, Step, Half-step if you're not in the UK!)

You can clearly see this in the neck diagram below and hear it as I play the C Major scale up the neck beginning on the root. This example is played over a C major chord (the first chord in the key of C Major) so you can hear the musical mood more clearly.

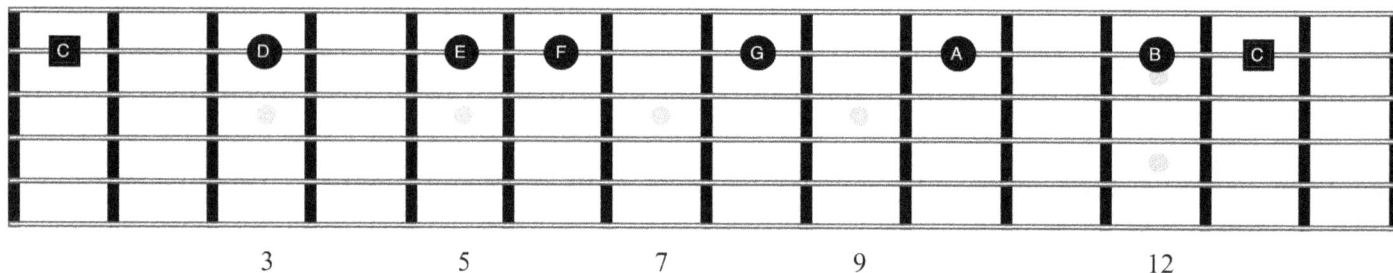

Example 1i:

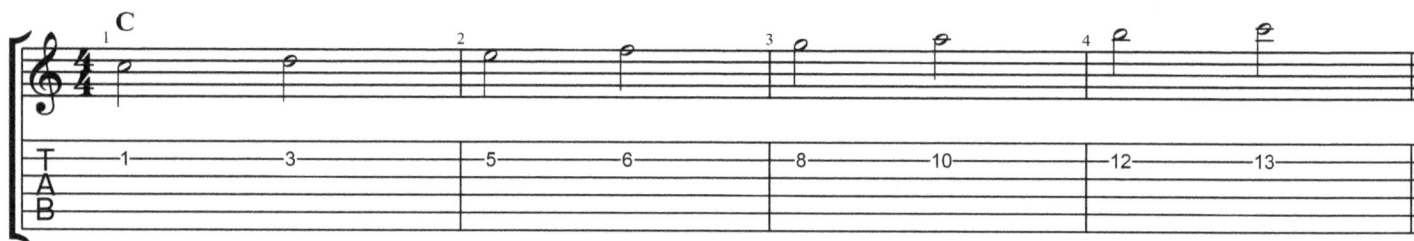

This pattern of tones and semitones in the major scale is the fundamental building block of pretty much all Western music for about the last 1,000 years and it's *so* important that it is given the *master formula* 1 2 3 4 5 6 7. This is literally the yardstick by which we describe *all* other scales.

It is important to understand that if you change this pattern of tones and semitones in any way, then you are no longer playing the major scale.

For example, if I play the notes C D *Eb* F G A B C, then I'm no longer playing the C Major scale, and the melodies and harmonies that this single Eb note introduces are massively different from those of the major scale. In fact, the scale I have created is the *melodic minor* scale.

When you *harmonize* (build a chord on) the first chord in C Major it contains the notes C E G to form a C Major chord.

When you harmonize the first note of the *melodic minor* scale (C D Eb F G A B C) it contains the notes C *Eb* and G to form a C *minor* chord, which is a completely different sound.

The Eb notes in this scale occur in various different chords and create a feel and musical effect that is startlingly different from C Major, considering you've changed just one note.

Returning to the idea that the C Major scale (C D E F G A B C) is our "master scale", with the formula 1 2 3 4 5 6 7, then the formula of this new melodic minor scale (C D *Eb* F G A B C) is described as 1 2 *b3* 4 5 6 7, because the third note (Eb) has been lowered by a semitone (half step).

This can be seen and heard clearly in the diagrams below.

C Major and C Melodic Minor:

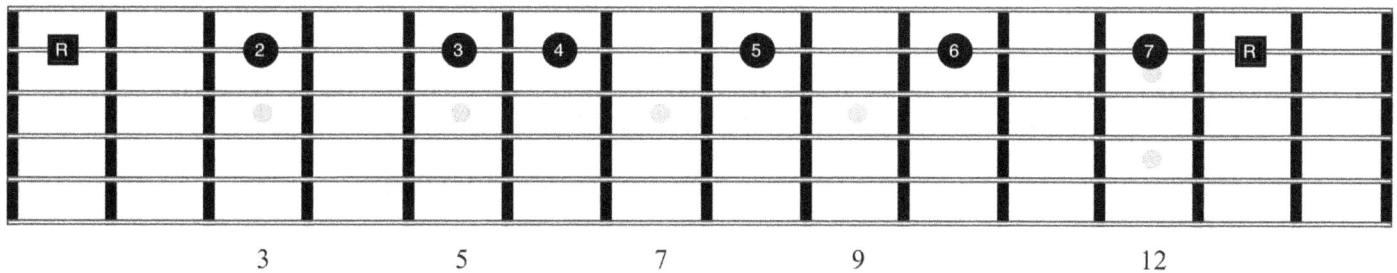

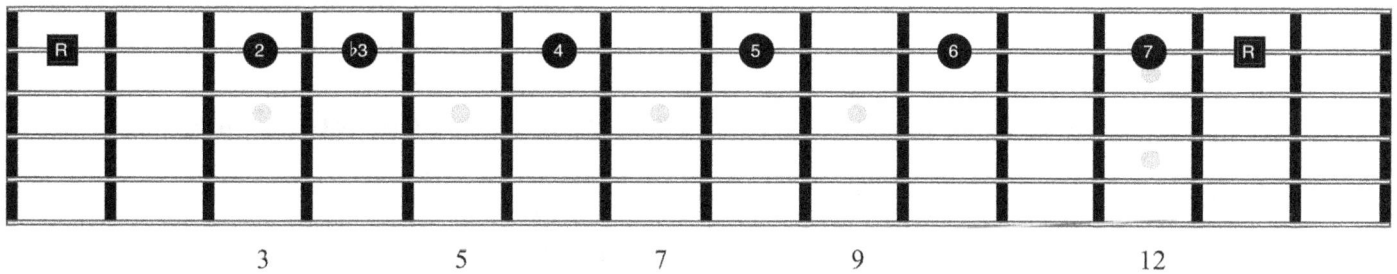

Example 1j:

It follows that you can alter any of the notes in the major scale formula to create a new scale/mode.

For example,

The formula 1 2 3 4 5 6 b7 (C D E F G A Bb) is the construction of the Mixolydian mode.

The formula 1 2 3 #4 5 6 7 (C D E F# G A B) is the construction of the Lydian mode.

The formula 1 2 b3 4 5 6 b7 (C D Eb F G A Bb) is the construction of the Dorian mode.

The formula 1 2 b3 4 5 b6 b7 (C D Eb F G Ab Bb) is the construction of the Aeolian mode.

Even though only one or two notes may change in the scale formula, the musical effect is normally massive.

Modes that contain a 3 (major third) are classed as major modes.

Modes that contain a b3 (minor third) interval are classed as *minor* modes.

Now we've covered the basics of scale construction, let's move on and take a detailed look at the Dorian mode and learn to see it around a musical pentatonic framework.

Chapter Two: From Minor Pentatonic to Dorian

Dorian is an important sound and is used in most types of music, including pop, dance, funk, soul, blues, and jazz. It is a minor mode because it contains a b3 interval, however it isn't as dark sounding as the Aeolian mode (natural minor scale) and creates a chilled-out musical vibe which has been used by pretty much every iconic guitarist you can name. As we work through this chapter you'll hear its "thoughtful, but not particularly sad sounding" vibe.

As you briefly saw in the introduction, to create a Dorian scale from a minor pentatonic scale we simply need to add two notes.

Here's a comparison of the A Minor Pentatonic and A Dorian scales.

Scale Notes	A	B	C	D	E	F#	G
Minor Pentatonic	1		b3	4	5		b7
Dorian Mode	1	2 (9)	b3	4	5	6 (13)	b7

As you can see, by adding the notes B and F# to the A Minor Pentatonic scale we create the A Dorian scale.

Let's remind ourselves what that looks like in the following diagram. You can hear both scales played over an A Dorian backing track in Example 2a

A Minor Pentatonic
Shape 1

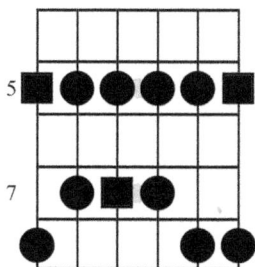

A Dorian
Shape 1

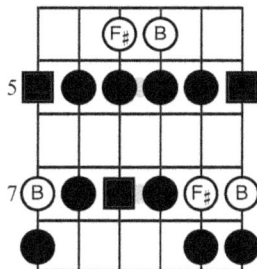

Example 2a:

As I mentioned in the introduction, when you start to use modal scales it's very easy for your playing to change from musically nuanced pentatonic soloing to a "cold" scale-playing approach where you quickly start running up and down scale patterns.

To avoid this kind of "scale thinking" we are going to use the minor pentatonic scale as our base and introduce the Dorian notes musically into our playing one at a time.

Let's start by introducing the note B, the 2nd/9th of the scale. This diagram shows the A Minor Pentatonic scale with the addition of the note B on the third string (4th fret)

A Minor Pentatonic
Shape 1

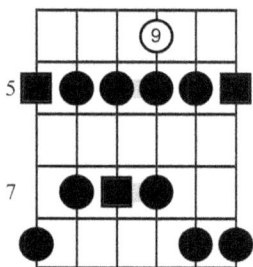

It's very important that you listen to the audio track and then use the A Dorian backing track to hear these sounds in a musical context. Remember, this is all about introducing new colours into your playing and you can only do that if you can hear what effect each note has.

Download the audio now from **www.fundamental-changes.com**

Begin by descending the A Minor Pentatonic scale and sliding into the note B on the third string. This is the 2nd (9th) note of the Dorian scale. Pause on this note before descending another two notes that are shared in common between A Minor Pentatonic and A Dorian.

Example 2b:

NB: From now on I'll be refer to 2nds as 9ths, 4ths as 11ths and 6ths as 13ths. You can see why in the following table.

The arpeggio notes (1, b3, 5 and b7) are named the same in both octaves, but the 2nd, 4th and 6th are named by their higher intervals.

Scale Note	A	B	C	D	E	F	G	A	B	C	D	E	F	G
Scale Interval	1	2	b3	4	5	6	b7	1/8	9	b3	11	5	13	b7

The next line ascends A Minor Pentatonic from the fifth string and again lands on the Dorian's 9th. I pause here before continuing up the notes that the two scales share.

Example 2c:

See how many simple pentatonic melodies you can create that land on the 9th of the scale before moving on to the following two examples. It's great practice to find as many routes as you can. Think about targeting the note by scale steps, jumping there from a distant note.

Spend at least 10 minutes doing this before learning the two short licks that follow. They consist of some more musical minor pentatonic ideas and add the 9th on the third string.

Example 2d:

Example 2e:

The 9th doesn't just live on the third string, of course. You can play it in a higher octave on the 7th fret of the first string too.

A Minor Pentatonic
Shape 1

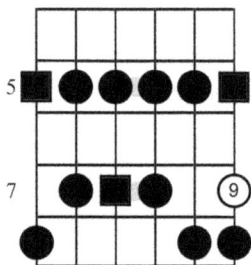

In this example I ascend the minor pentatonic scale from the 3rd string to land on the 9th and finish off the phrase with a couple of pentatonic notes.

Example 2f:

This idea again lands on the higher 9th but this time from above. I ascend A Minor Pentatonic from the third string all the way to the 8th fret on the top string, then descend a half-step to land on the 7th fret before finishing off the line melodically.

Example 2g:

Again, spend a while finding how many ways you can target this higher 9th before moving onto the following three licks. These ideas add some bends and slides to the minor pentatonic scale and highlight the 9th on the high E string.

Example 2h:

Example 2i:

The pentatonic phrase below includes the 9th in both octaves.

Example 2j:

The other interval we add to the minor pentatonic scale to create the Dorian mode is the 6th (13th). In the key of A, that note is F# and is located on the 4th fret of the fourth string.

A Minor Pentatonic
Shape 1

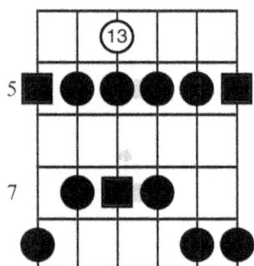

Try descending A Minor Pentatonic from the second string and slide into the Dorian 13th. Let it ring to hear its effect on the melody, before finishing off the line with a musical idea.

Example 2k:

Now ascend A Minor Pentatonic to land on the 13th in the same location. Again, the line below lets the 13th ring before finishing off with a musical phrase.

Example 2l:

See how many ways you can find to target the 13th before learning these two short pentatonic licks that incorporate the 13th into a musical phrase.

Example 2m:

Example 2n:

The 13th can also be played at the 14th fret on the first string. Begin at the top of the minor pentatonic shape, descend to the 13th and continue into the Dorian mode.

A Minor Pentatonic
Shape 4

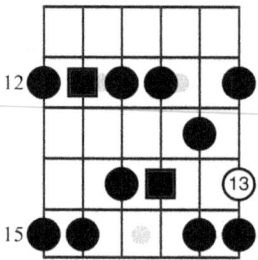

Example 2o:

This line ascends to the 13th and transitions into a Dorian melody.

Example 2p:

See how many ways you can find to target this note then transition into a Dorian scale idea. When you're ready, try these pentatonic lines that introduce bluesy phrasing ideas and add the Dorian 13th in a more natural way.

Example 2q:

Example 2r:

Now you know the locations of the 9th and 13th notes that are added to the minor pentatonic scale, it's easy to fluidly add them both into your phrases. The following two licks give you a starting point to create some melodic ideas that contain them both.

Example 2s:

Example 2t:

Do remember that while you *can* add both these notes to the minor pentatonic scale, you don't *have* to. In fact, you can get extremely melodic results by being selective. Jam for 30 minutes playing minor pentatonic ideas and just add the 9th, then solo for 30 minutes and just add the 13th to see what you can come up with.

The overarching point is that simply *thinking* of Dorian as a minor pentatonic scale with two added notes reduces your tendency to start playing full (and often mindless) Dorian scale runs over grooves. It encourages you to be a bit more thoughtful about your note choice. You can already play melodically with the pentatonic scale, so by using it as a framework for your solos your lines will stay "pentatonic-y" but introduce the richer Dorian colours.

If I had just given you a full note-map of the Dorian scale and asked you to jam with it over the backing track, you'd probably have started playing up and down the scale, maybe tried to add speed, maybe introduced some scale sequences, and kind of "draped" the scale over the whole solo.

By focusing on using the minor pentatonic as a strong melodic framework that underpins our lines, then dropping in Dorian notes in a more mindful way, you automatically begin to play more musically. In fact, you sound more like a melodic, thoughtful guitarist. This approach is a great way to begin a solo because by thinking like this, it's easy to create the seed of an idea that gradually builds into more complex melodic material as the solo progresses. In essence, you immediately think *melody*, and not "here are all the notes I can play, let's shred!"

We've learned the higher placements of the Dorian 9ths and 13ths and the diagram below shows these in relation to the A Minor Pentatonic shape one box. The pentatonic scale is shown with black dots and the Dorian notes are added with hollow dots. You'll notice I haven't covered the 9ths and 13ths on the lower strings in this chapter because you'll probably spend most of your time soloing in the higher range of the guitar. However, you should know where these notes are too, so take time to learn them in the same way as before.

Learn this scale shape ascending and descending from the lowest to the highest note.

A Dorian
Shape 1

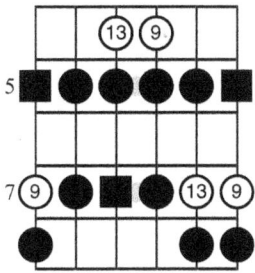

To round off the chapter, here are three longer lines that begin as pentatonic ideas, gradually introduce one or two Dorian notes, transition into busier Dorian scale ideas, then return to a strong pentatonic phrase to finish.

Notice that I play melodically and use bends, slides and vibrato freely to make the lines vocal and musical.

Example 2u:

Am

```
       full      full
   8—5       8—5—8—5              7—5                                       
      8        8        8—5          8—5—10   8—5       5—7—5—    5—          
                                              7               7      7—5—4—  
                                                                          5—7—
```

Example 2v:

Am

```
   5—8—5—   5—8—5—   5—8—5—      5—7—5—                                          
         8        8        8         8—5—8—5—   5     7—5—   5—7—5—   5—          
                                              7          7        7      7—5—    
                                                                             5—7—
```

Example 2w:

Chapter Three: Dorian Continued

As you've heard, using the minor pentatonic scale as a framework to introduce modal colours musically works really well. In the previous chapter we added 9th and 13th intervals to the first position of the A Minor Pentatonic scale to create the A Dorian mode. I'm guessing that this is a position you already know and love on the guitar. But what about other areas of the neck?

In this chapter I'm going to teach you how to add Dorian intervals to the four remaining minor pentatonic shapes. I'll focus in detail on shape four of the A Minor Pentatonic scale as it's a favourite of many guitarists and is an easily accessible soloing area. Once we've looked in detail at shape four, I'll show you the three other pentatonic positions and you'll quickly be able to repeat the process for each shape.

We will finish off with a couple of useful licks that transition from pentatonic to Dorian in each position to get your musical exploration started. However, I do stress that it's much more important to begin by learning one or two areas of the fretboard well, rather than trying to quickly cover the neck for the sake of it. There are countless guitarists out there who just use position one scale shapes and still sound excellent. If you remember to think "music before theory" it'll help you to spend more time exploring one position before moving on.

Let's get started.

Shape four of the A Minor Pentatonic scale is played up around the 12th fret of the fretboard and looks like this. The root is on the fifth string at the 12th fret.

A Minor Pentatonic
Shape 4

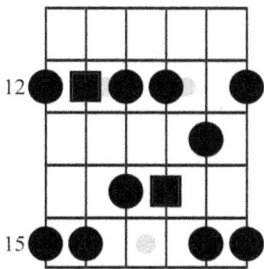

Example 3a:

When you have memorised this shape, we can begin to add the Dorian notes to the shape beginning with the 9th.

The first 9th (the note B) lives at the 12th fret on the second string.

A Minor Pentatonic
Shape 4

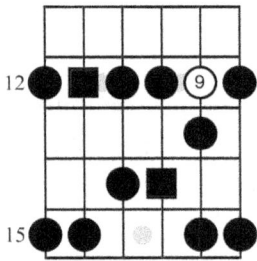

Play through this descending A Minor Pentatonic idea that lands on the 9th then continues down the pentatonic scale.

Example 3b:

This idea ascends to the same 9th from the fourth string and continues up the scale.

Example 3c:

There's another 9th an octave below on the 14th fret of the fifth string. This idea descends to target it with an *enclosure* before continuing the melodic line.

A Minor Pentatonic
Shape 4

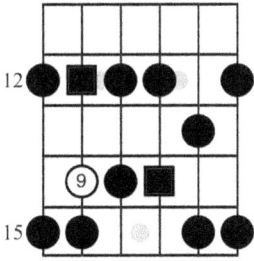

Example 3d:

See how many simple pentatonic melodies you can create that incorporate the Dorian 9th before moving on to the following two examples. It's great practice to find as many routes as you can. Think about targeting the note by scale steps, jumping there from a distance, or even by bending into it. For example, you could bend the 14th fret on the third string up a tone to sound like the 12th fret on the second.

When you've explored as many simple routes into the 9th as you can, learn this lick that has many pentatonic nuances but incorporates the 9th of the scale to hint at the Dorian mode.

Example 3e:

Now let's add the 13th of the Dorian mode (the note F#) to the A Minor Pentatonic scale. It's located on the 11th fret of the G string.

Here's a simple pentatonic line that ascends into the 13th. However, we're going to make a slight change to our approach here. Instead of continuing up the pure A Minor Pentatonic scale after playing the Dorian 13th, we will also include the 9th on the second string that we learned in Example 3a, before ending on the b3rd of A Minor Pentatonic.

By doing this, we have transitioned smoothly from Minor Pentatonic into a short section of the full Dorian mode by including both the 9th and 13th of the scale.

Example 3f:

```
Am
1                                                   2
T--------------------------------12----14----11----12---|-14--------12----13----15----12----13-------------|
A------------12----14------------------------------------|---------------------------------------------14---|
B--12----15---------------------------------------------|--------------------------------------------------|
```

This idea descends into the 13th then continues down the pure A Minor Pentatonic scale for a few notes.

Example 3g:

```
Am
1                                              2
T--15----12-------------------------------------|--------------------------------------------------|
A--------------15----13----14----12----11----12-|--14----12--------------------------------------|
B----------------------------------------------|--------------14----12----15----12---------------|
```

There is also a 13th located on the 14th fret of the high E string. This first line ascends through the pentatonic scale to land there, pauses, then resolves with a couple of notes from the minor pentatonic scale.

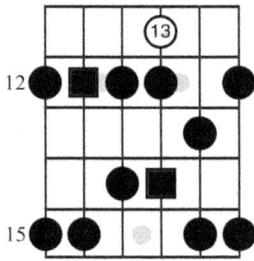

A Minor Pentatonic
Shape 4

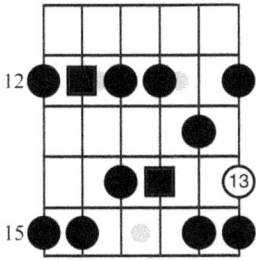

Example 3h:

Am

This example also ascends the pentatonic scale but uses an enclosure to target the 13th from a half step above before continuing.

Example 3i:

Am

The next line begins with a big, bold 9th (B) on the second string before continuing with a pentatonic phrase that remains influenced by that colour.

Example 3j:

Similarly, this idea begins with a strong 13th before continuing with a phrase that is mainly pentatonic.

Example 3k:

This lick begins in A Minor Pentatonic but uses the 9th to transition into a more Dorian based scale idea that later includes the 13th.

Example 3l:

Here's a similar idea that uses the 13th to transition from A Minor Pentatonic to a fuller A Dorian melody that includes the 9th.

Example 3m:

The diagram below shows the Dorian mode built around shape four of the A Minor Pentatonic scale. I've marked the pentatonic notes in black and the Dorian notes with hollow circles.

You'll see that there are a couple of notes added on the lower strings that we didn't cover in detail above. In this chapter I've focused on the higher notes in the scale because they are the ones you'll use most commonly in your solos, but of course you should learn the whole scale in the same way.

A Dorian
Shape 4

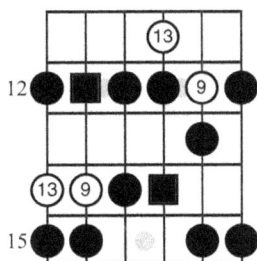

Here are four lines that transition naturally from A Minor Pentatonic shape four to A Dorian and back. I've added typical "guitarry" playing nuances like bends, slides and legato to make the phrases more musical.

Example 3n:

Example 3o:

Example 3p:

Example 3q:

Here are two lines that begin with a big bold Dorian note which his followed by a pentatonic idea that includes a couple of Dorian intervals.

Example 3r:

Example 3s:

Try creating similar ideas to the ones above by using the possible frameworks listen below.

Begin with simple scale ideas and play more interesting phrases as you get more confident. Don't forget to add bends, slides, vibrato, legato… any of the tricks that make the guitar sound more vocal. Remember, the idea is to think of pentatonic phrasing but either target or gradually introduce Dorian intervals to create a richer sound.

Spend time learning how to *feel* the difference in mood created by actively targeting the 9th, targeting the 13th, and by including them both in a phrase. Throughout, you should always be "thinking" of pentatonic phrasing with Dorian notes added around it.

Here are some possible structures to practice this exercise:

1) Simple pentatonic phrase > target a single Dorian note > pentatonic idea + Dorian note

2) Single Dorian note > transition into pentatonic idea without Dorian note

3) Single Dorian note > transition into pentatonic idea with Dorian note

4) Simple pentatonic phrase that includes a single Dorian note

5) Simple pentatonic phrase that includes both Dorian notes

6) Simple pentatonic phrase > target a single Dorian note and use it to transition into a full Dorian idea

While you could (and hopefully will) spend a lifetime exploring shapes one and four of the Dorian mode, I want to briefly cover the other three positions we've not touched on yet.

By now I'm sure you're getting the idea of how to practice targeting/introducing Dorian notes into pentatonic phrases. If not, here's a brief recap:

- Learn the minor pentatonic shape

- Observe where the Dorian 9ths are located in the shape using the diagrams provided

- Play simple pentatonic scale ideas that ascend and descend into each 9th

- Play more musical lick-based pentatonic ideas that incorporate the 9th

- Observe where the Dorian 13ths are located in the shape

- Play simple pentatonic scale ideas that ascend and descend into each 13th

- Play more musical lick-based pentatonic ideas that incorporate the 13th

- Create phrases that have the following structure: begin with a pentatonic idea, transition into Dorian by incorporating the 9th or 13th intervals (or both). Later, explore by moving into more Dorian-heavy ideas, then return to minor pentatonic phrases

As Dorian might be new to you, I want to give you a couple of short, specifically Dorian phrases you can use if you get stuck improvising with the scale. You can use these as more intricate ideas as you get deeper into your exploration.

I'll teach them to you in shape four but use your ears and translate them into the other shapes of the Dorian mode. They are all strong phrases you can use to get yourself started with Dorian.

The first two phrases begin on the 9th of A Dorian (the note B).

Example 3t:

Example 3u:

The next two phrases begin on the 13th of A Dorian (the note F#).

Example 3v:

Example 3w:

I highly recommend you spend your time exploring this process using just shape one and shape four of the Dorian scale, but when you're ready to dive in, here are all five positions of Dorian to explore when you're ready.

As before, learn the dark dots of the pentatonic scale first, then go through the steps in this and the previous chapter to gradually introduce the hollow dots of the Dorian mode. Have fun!

A Dorain
Shape 1

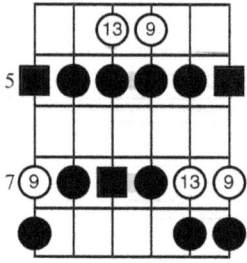

A Dorian
Shape 2

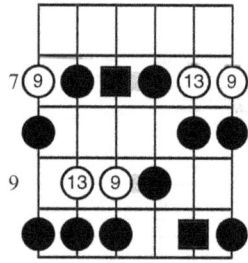

A Dorian
Shape 3

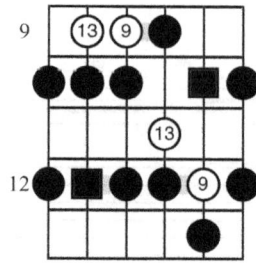

A Dorian
Shape 4

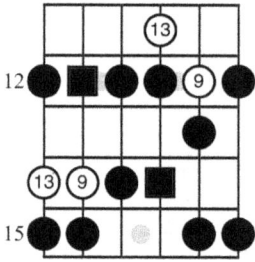

A Dorian
Shape 5

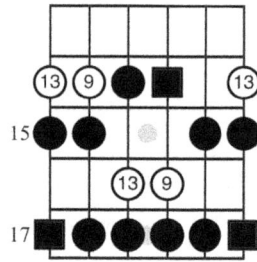

Chapter Four: From Minor Pentatonic to Aeolian

The Aeolian mode (or Natural Minor scale), is one of the most important scales for guitarists as, alongside the minor pentatonic scale, it creates the quintessential sound of rock and heavy metal. From Black Sabbath to Deep Purple, Metallica to Rage Against the Machine, Jimi Hendrix to AC/DC, everyone you care to name has used the Aeolian mode to create music on the harder side of rock.

As we briefly touched on in the introduction, the Aeolian only has one note (the 13th) different from the Dorian mode. While people often find it surprising that changing a single note in a scale has such a profound effect on it, the difference in mood between Dorian and Aeolian is almost literally, night and day... well, night and evening anyway. While Dorian delivers a kind of late evening jazzy sophistication, Aeolian evokes church bells ringing out the midnight chimes while vampires battle in the moonlight. Or something. Your mileage may vary.

As I mentioned, there is only a one note difference between the Dorian and Aeolian scales. While A Dorian contains a nice, light natural 13th, A Aeolian contains a darker b13 which gives it its rockier vibe.

The formula for Dorian is 1 2 b3 4 5 **6** b7

The formula for Aeolian is 1 2 b3 4 5 **b6** b7

This means that when we build Aeolian around A Minor Pentatonic, the natural 9th we introduced in the previous chapters (remember, the 9th is the same as the 2nd) is exactly the same. In fact, there are only a few scales you'll ever use which contain a b9 (Phrygian, Phrygian Dominant and, if you're feeling brave, Locrian!)

That's great news because you already learned the locations of the natural 9ths around the minor pentatonic scale in the previous chapter.

So, building the Aeolian mode around the minor pentatonic scale is now all about locating the b13 (the b13 is the same as the b6), and it should be no surprise that the b13 lives just a half-step below the natural 13.

To quickly summarise all of this, by adding the 9th and b13th (the notes B and F) to the A Minor Pentatonic scale we create the A Aeolian mode.

Scale Notes	A	B	C	D	E	F	G
Minor Pentatonic	1		b3	4	5		b7
Aeolian Mode	1	2 (9)	b3	4	5	b6 (b13)	b7

Let's see what that looks like in the following diagram. You can hear these scales both played over an A Aeolian backing track in Example 4a

A Minor Pentatonic
Shape 1

A Aeolian
Shape 1

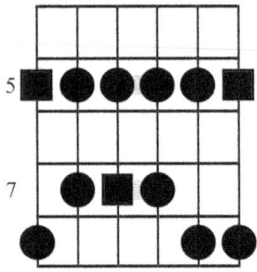

Example 4a:

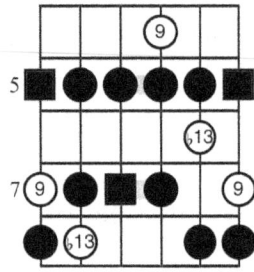

Let's learn to target the b13 note (F) on the second string.

A Minor Pentatonic
Shape 1

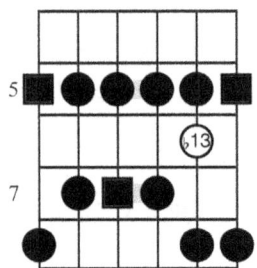

We'll start off simply by ascending the minor pentatonic scale to land on the F at the 6th fret. Let it ring to hear how this affects the mood of the melody.

Example 4b:

Now let's begin in the same way but this time continue moving the melody forward after landing on the b13. You'll hear that the b13 creates a slight melodic *tension* against the backing chords and wants to *resolve* to another note in the scale. A classical musician would tell you that it should fall to the 5th of the scale, but we're modern rock guitarists so we aren't too bothered about that.

Example 4c:

Let's reverse this idea and begin a phrase with a sustained b13th that resolves to a descending minor pentatonic scale line.

Example 4d:

This line begins in the minor pentatonic scale above the b13 and uses an enclosure to target it before transitioning into a phrase that involves a few more A Aeolian notes.

Example 4e:

Am

```
full
T  -8--5--6----5---------------------5-----|  -8--5--6----5--6--5----------|  -5----------|
A  ----------7--5----------5--7=-5--8-------|  ------------------7-------|  --7--5-------|
B  ----------------7--5-7--------------------|  --------------------------|  --------7---|
```

Let's explore a few more lick-based ideas around the b13 on the second string. Play this bluesy A Minor Pentatonic bending idea that uses the b13 as a transitioning point into more A Aeolian territory.

Example 4f:

Am

```
        full   full              full                                              full
T  ----5----5------------------5--8--5--6----8-------|  -8--6--5----6--5--------|  ----5-------|
A  -7----7----7--5-----------7-----------------------|  ----------7-------7--5--|  -7----5-----|
B  -------------------7-------7-------------------5---|  ------------------------|  --------7---|
```

This line *sequences* notes from the A Minor Pentatonic scale and again transitions via the b13 into a sequenced Aeolian idea.

Example 4g:

Am

```
T  --------------------5----------6--5--8--6----5---8--7----5---|  -8--5--------------|
A  --------5-----7----5----5---7--------------8--------------8--|  -----7--5--------5-|
B  -----7----5-7---7-----------7-----------------------------------|  --------7--5--7---7-|
```

The other b13 is located on the fifth string at the 8th fret. While it's low in the scale, you should still be able to see it in conjunction with the minor pentatonic. Our first approach is to descend the A Minor Pentatonic scale and land on this note.

A Minor Pentatonic
Shape 1

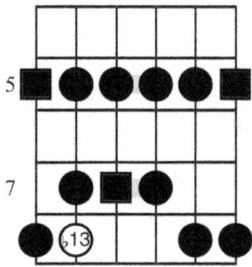

Example 4h:

Here's a more melodic pentatonic line that descends to the fifth string b13 and incorporates it into a more musical line.

Repeat the process shown in the earlier examples and learn to target this lower b13.

Let's move on and introduce the Aeolian 9th in the first position of the pentatonic mode.

As you spent a lot of time targeting this note for Dorian in Chapter Two, you should be good at this by now and we can miss out a lot of the steps.

We'll immediately start by playing a scale-based pentatonic line that targets the 9th (B) on the first string, then descends through the pentatonic scale and also includes the b13 (F) on the second string.

A Minor Pentatonic
Shape 1

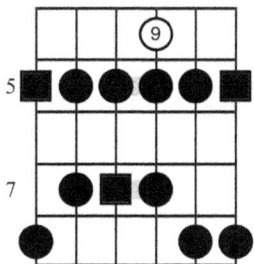

Example 4i:

Next try this ascending line and use an enclosure to target the 9th. The line descends through the scale and also includes the b13 on the second string.

Example 4j:

This line starts with a big, bold 9th and then moves into more minor pentatonic territory but still adds the b13 to the melody.

Example 4k:

Here are two more musical licks the freely move between minor pentatonic and Aeolian ideas.

Example 4l:

Example 4m:

The other 9th is located on the third string at the 4th fret. This line ascends the pentatonic scale to target it then continues ascending to rest on the b13 before finishing off the idea.

A Minor Pentatonic
Shape 1

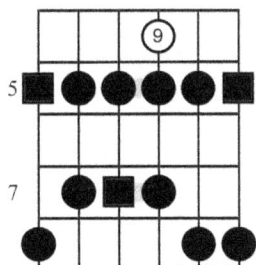

Example 4n:

This idea descends through the pentatonic scale to the same 9th then ascends to include the b13 on the second string.

Example 4o:

OK, now you're getting the hang of this, I'm going to show you a new exercise you can use to practice your scale transitions.

You'll begin by playing from the highest note (C) in A Minor Pentatonic shape one, then descend the scale for four 1/8th notes.

From there, you will switch to the next closest note in the A Aeolian mode and continue down the Aeolian scale. Remember, a lot of Aeolian notes are in the pentatonic scale so don't panic if you play another pentatonic note.

In this case, you would have ended up on the 5th fret of the second string, so the next Aeolian note is the 7th fret of the third string. From there, continue down the Aeolian scale for four 1/8th notes then switch to the next closest note in the minor pentatonic scale.

Keep going and descend all the way to the bottom of the shape before ascending again in the same way.

This exercise should be played at a slow speed as it requires a lot of concentration.

Here are four bars of what that exercise might look like beginning from C. However, it's great practice to begin from any point in the scale.

Example 4p:

Once you've got the hang of that, repeat the exercise again but this time play a little bit more freely and target scale notes that are simply close by as you change scale. You don't have to keep ascending or descending in one direction, simply move to a close note of the next scale and continue from there.

For example, this exercise begins from C again, but when I've descended four notes of A Minor Pentatonic, instead of descending again like in the previous example, I "grab" the F on the 6th fret a half-step above where I finish. From there I decide to continue descending the Aeolian scale for four notes, although I could have ascended. Example 4q shows this freer approach over four bars. As I'm free to transition into different notes, you'll hear this exercise sounds a bit more musical because it is more led by my ears.

Example 4q:

Another musical idea to help you target the Aeolian colour tones is to bend into them from a pentatonic note below. This approach works on any mode, so go back and try it on Dorian in the previous chapters. This first idea plays with a short pentatonic idea then bends the 5th of the scale up a half-step to hit the b6 of Aeolian on the second string.

Example 4r:

This line begins with an A Minor Pentatonic scale tone then bends that note a whole step to become the natural 9th. Because of the position of the note on the top string this bend might be a bit of a challenge, so don't be afraid to change hand position and use your third finger for the bend, as this will give you more strength and control.

Example 4s:

Let's end this section with four licks that move between A Minor Pentatonic and A Aeolian more naturally to create a melodic set of phrases. These lines include plenty of expressive techniques such as bends, vibrato, double-stops and legato. Notice how I occasionally bend up from notes in one scale to target notes in the other. For example, the root of the pentatonic scale can be bent up to the natural 9th. The natural 9th can be bent up to the b3. The 5th can be bent to the b13, etc. We can also use *pre-bends* to target a note then release the bend to return to more common ground.

Example 4t:

Example 4u:

Example 4v:

Example 4w:

Now it's over to you.

Spend as much time as you can transitioning between A Minor Pentatonic and A Aeolian in this position, and improvise over the jam tracks. If you get stuck soloing with Aeolian, the final three licks in this chapter are short phrases that are entirely Aeolian and begin on either a 9th or b13th. You can use them as a starting point for your Aeolian explorations.

Remember to use the structures outlined in the previous chapter to practice switching between scales. I'll repeat them after the following three Aeolian ideas.

Example 4x:

Example 4y:

Example 4z:

Soloing Strategies:

1) Simple pentatonic phrase > target a single Aeolian note > pentatonic idea + Aeolian note

2) Single Aeolian note > transition into pentatonic idea without Aeolian note

3) Single Aeolian note > transition into pentatonic idea with Aeolian note

4) Simple pentatonic phrase that includes a single Aeolian note

5) Simple pentatonic phrase that includes both Aeolian notes

6) Simple pentatonic phrase > target a single Aeolian note and use it to transition into a full Aeolian idea

In the next chapter we will examine how to move from minor pentatonic to Aeolian in shape four.

Chapter Five: Aeolian Continued

As with Dorian, your priority should always be to develop a deep connection with the notes of the scale in Aeolian shape one. However, as you progress you will obviously want to solo in higher parts of the neck. The next most common position to learn is shape four and we will begin this chapter by learning how A Aeolian fits around that minor pentatonic scale shape.

As you learned in the previous chapter, Aeolian and Dorian only have one note difference between them. They both share all the notes of the minor pentatonic scale along with a natural 9th. The only difference is that Dorian has a natural 13th and Aeolian has a b13th.

As you've already covered the locations of the natural 9ths, the first interval to learn to add to the minor pentatonic scale in this position is the b13.

Here's a diagram of the shape four A Minor Pentatonic scale with the Aeolian notes marked with hollow dots. The root is on the fifth string at the 12th fret.

A Aeolian
Shape 4

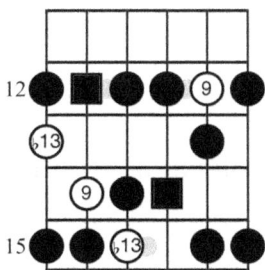

Example 5a:

As you can see, the highest b13 (F) is located on the top string at the 13th fret. Let's play through some pentatonic scale ideas that target it. We will begin simply with an ascending line that lands on the b13.

A Minor Pentatonic
Shape 4

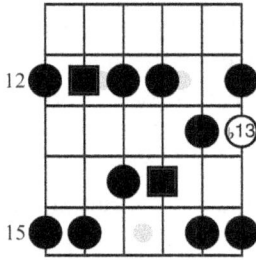

Example 5b:

This line ascends up to the 15th fret and then drops down to target the b13 before resolving back to the pentatonic scale

Example 5c:

Now for something a little more musical. It begins with a short bluesy phrase that targets the b13 then returns to a pentatonic idea.

Example 5d:

The next idea transitions from a minor pentatonic scale phrase into a full Aeolian idea using the same b13 as a pivot point. Notice how I include the natural 9th in the continuation.

Example 5e:

The other useful b13 is on the 15th fret of the fourth string. It's a little low but it's worth knowing. This descending pentatonic scale line targets the note, pauses, then re-ascends the pentatonic scale.

A Minor Pentatonic
Shape 4

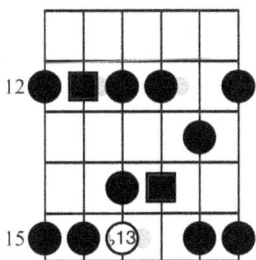

Example 5f:

Here's a more realistic and musical way to incorporate the lower b13 into a pentatonic idea.

Example 5g:

Finally, for now, this phrase uses the lower b13 to transition from a full pentatonic to a full Aeolian lick. Again, see how I include the natural 9th.

Example 5h:

Here's an idea that begins with a bold b13 in the higher octave that moves into more standard pentatonic territory.

Example 5i:

Even though you've previously learned the locations of the natural 9th in relation to Dorian, it's important to learn them in conjunction with Aeolian, even though they are in the same place. This is because the slightly differing shape of the scale can be a little disorientating.

The most useful 9th (the note B) is located on the 12th fret of the second string. This A Minor Pentatonic idea ascends the scale and adds it to the melody.

A Minor Pentatonic
Shape 4

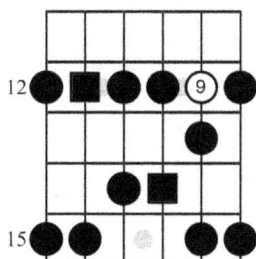

Example 5j:

This line descends the minor pentatonic scale more melodically and targets the 9th before resolving the phrase.

Example 5k:

So far so good!

There was nothing in the previous two examples that you didn't cover when studying Dorian earlier. However, this time we are going to play a bluesy pentatonic phrase, transition into the Aeolian via the 9th, then play another bluesy pentatonic idea that incorporates both the 9th and the b13.

Example 5l:

Here's another melodic idea that takes the same approach.

Example 5m:

In the next four licks, I want to show you a melodic trick that beautifully enhances this pentatonic to modal approach. We will use bends to move between Aeolian and pentatonic notes.

In the first lick, I will play a phrase that lands on the natural 5th of A Minor Pentatonic, then bend it up a half step to target the Aeolian b13.

Example 5n:

The next line bends the root of the minor pentatonic scale up a tone to hit the natural 9th on the third string.

Example 5o:

Let's reverse the previous idea and try this lick, which bends from the natural 9th of Aeolian up to the b3 that is in both scales.

Example 5p:

This line combines the two approaches and uses multiple bends to target the b3, 9th, and b13.

Example 5q:

You can (and should) spend hours exploring this approach as bending in and out of target notes will really help you hear how these modal intervals affect the sound of the pentatonic scale. Go back and try this with Aeolian shape one from the previous chapter, and with Dorian too. In Dorian, the natural 13 bends up nicely by a half-step to target the b7.

To practice the ideas in this chapter, return to the soloing structures we discussed in the previous chapters. These were:

1) Simple pentatonic phrase > target a single Aeolian note > pentatonic idea + Aeolian note

2) Single Aeolian note > transition into pentatonic idea without Aeolian note

3) Single Aeolian note > transition into pentatonic idea with Aeolian note

4) Simple pentatonic phrase that includes a single Aeolian note

5) Simple pentatonic phrase that includes both Aeolian notes

6) Simple pentatonic phrase > target a single Aeolian note and use it to transition into a full Aeolian idea

Also, don't forget to the practice the "four notes of pentatonic, four notes of Aeolian" exercise we looked at earlier.

The following three examples show you some "pure" Aeolian vocabulary you can use as a starting point to build your phrasing in the Aeolian part of these structures. The real secret is to simply put on the backing track and explore as much as you can.

Example 5r:

Example 5s:

Example 5t:

Example 5u:

Finally, here are three "kitchen sink" licks that go to town on this concept. I might start with an A Minor Pentatonic idea, an Aeolian note, an Aeolian scale lick, or a blend of both. Your job is to use your ears to hear which is which. I want you to listen carefully and focus on hearing the transitions between the two scales as I make them as smooth as possible. Remember: "Pentatonic phasing with modal colours".

Example 5v:

Example 5w:

Example 5x:

We've covered melodic ideas in shapes one and four of Aeolian, and once again you should spend most of your time exploring these. However, there are of course three other locations you can play Aeolian on the guitar neck and I've included these below.

As always, pentatonic scales are shown with dark dots and Aeolian notes are shown with hollow dots. Learn the pentatonic scales first and repeat the steps in this chapter to add one Aeolian note at a time.

Your practice time should always be spent finding creative ways to use pentatonic phrasing while introducing one or both modal notes smoothly and creatively. Bending is a beautiful melodic tool so study the maps to see where you can bend from one scale to another, whether that's from pentatonic to Aeolian, or vice versa.

A Aeolian
Shape 1

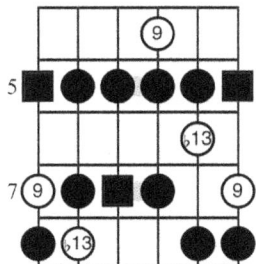

A Aeolian
Shape 2

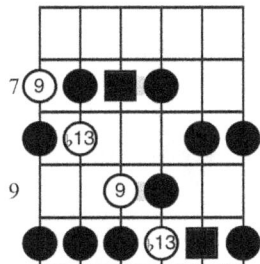

A Aeolian
Shape 3

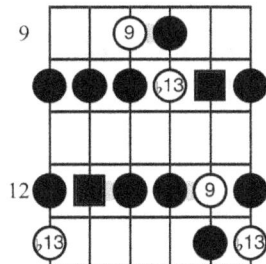

A Aeolian
Shape 4

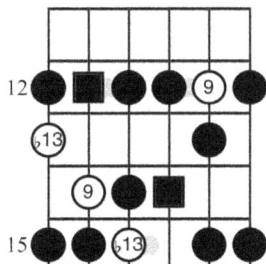

A Aeolian
Shape 5

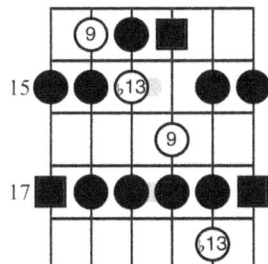

Chapter Six: From Major Pentatonic to Mixolydian

We've explored two of the most common minor scales for guitarists, so let's now turn our attention to a couple of useful major-type scales. We'll begin with a look at Mixolydian because it's a great gateway between major and minor musical territory.

Mixolydian is used frequently in blues, country and rock, and is the fifth mode of the major scale. It has a similar construction to the major scale, the only difference being that Mixolydian contains a b7 which gives it a cooler, more chilled sound. The b7 interval fits perfectly with a dominant 7 chord formula (1 3 5 b7) so Mixolydian works great over dominant 7, 9, 11, and 13 chords.

When you compare the formulas of the major and Mixolydian scales you'll quickly see the difference:

Major: 1 2 3 4 5 6 7

Mixolydian: 1 2 3 4 5 6 b7

As Mixolydian is classed as a major mode (it contains a major 3rd) we will first learn it in conjunction with the *major* pentatonic scale. However, it is so common to combine Mixolydian with the minor pentatonic scale that we will learn it around the minor pentatonic shape in the next chapter.

Let's begin by learning shape one of the A Major Pentatonic scale. If this is new to you, spend some time memorizing it.

A Major Pentatonic
Shape 1

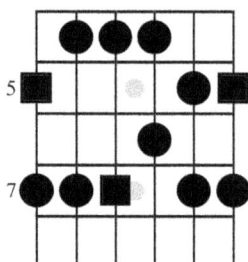

Example 6a:

Take a moment to compare the major pentatonic and Mixolydian formulas. You will see that once again we only need to add two notes, the 4th and b7th to the major pentatonic to create the full Mixolydian mode.

Scale Notes	A	B	C#	D	E	F	G
Major Pentatonic	1	2	3		5	6	
Mixolydian Mode	1	2	3	4 (11)	5	6	b7

Check out the diagram below that shows the Mixolydian scale around the major pentatonic framework.

A Mixolydian
Shape 1

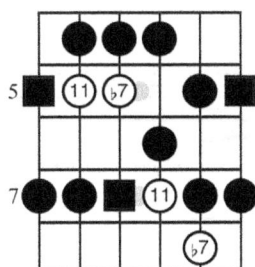

Let's start by finding ways to add just the b7 to the major pentatonic scale. The highest b7 in the scale is located on the 8th fret of the second string.

Begin from the fourth string root of A Major Pentatonic and ascend the scale to the root on the first string while adding the b7 on the second string.

A Major Pentatonic
Shape 1

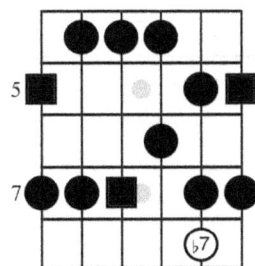

Example 6b:

This example reverses the previous run.

Example 6c:

The next pentatonic line to incorporate the b7 begins from the 5th fret of the second string.

Example 6d:

This idea begins from the 3rd of the scale on the third string, 6th fret.

Example 6e:

Spend time creating some simple lines that ascend or descend the A Major Pentatonic scale and include the b7 on the second string. Explore the scale over the Mixolydian backing track and see where your ears take you. Remember, you can always bend from the 6th on the 6th fret up a half step to target the b7.

The other b7 in this shape is located on the 5th fret of the fourth string. Here are four simple scale based lines that ascend or descend into it over the Mixolydian backing track.

A Major Pentatonic
Shape 1

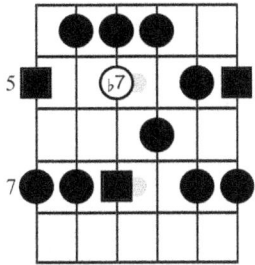

Example 6f:

Example 6g:

Example 6h:

Example 6i:

The following examples are more musical lines that use the major pentatonic scale with an added b7. I've added bends, plus the usual expressive techniques and melodic jumps to make them more melodic. You might still think these lines sound a little bit forced… and you'd be right! – the real art of using Mixolydian is to combine it with the minor pentatonic scale as well as the major pentatonic, so have a little patience and we will look at these types of lines in the next chapter.

Example 6j:

Example 6k:

Example 6l:

OK, now you're starting to get the feel of this scale, let's add the 4th/11th into the mix. The highest 11th is located on the 7th fret of the third string. We'll lose the b7th for now and look at three simple melodic ideas that are exclusively major pentatonic with the added 11th.

You'll immediately hear that "major pentatonic plus an 11th" has quite a different vibe than "major pentatonic plus b7".

A Major Pentatonic
Shape 1

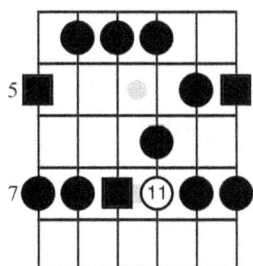

Example 6m:

Example 6n:

Example 6o:

The other 4th/11th is located on the 5th fret of the fifth string. It's useful to know, even though it's a bit low down in the scale. Here are two scale-based lines that target it. The first descends from the 3rd of the scale.

A Major Pentatonic
Shape 1

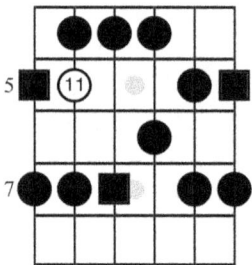

Example 6p:

This line ascends through the 11th from below.

Example 6q:

The final four lines in this section are more natural and combine both the 11th and the b7 interchangeably with the major pentatonic scale. There are plenty of places where you can bend in and out of the pentatonic scale. For example, you might see the following ideas:

- Play the b7 and bend to the root

- Play the 3rd and bend to the 11th

- Play the 6th and bend to the b7

- Play the 11th and bend to the 5th (less common)

Learn the lines below then come up with your own licks that include these kinds of bends. Remember, the approach is to "think" about major pentatonic phrasing and then add Mixolydian colour tones. Don't start mindlessly running up and down the Mixolydian scale!

Example 6r:

Example 6s:

Example 6t:

Example 6u:

In this chapter we've taken a very "pure" approach to playing the Mixolydian scale. In the next section, we're going to get a bit dirtier and learn how it fits around the minor pentatonic scale. This might feel counterintuitive as we've already learned that Mixolydian is a major-type mode. However, most of the best Mixolydian material comes from this interplay between major and minor. We'll learn how in the next chapter.

Chapter Seven: From Minor Pentatonic to Mixolydian

As the Mixolydian scale contains a major 3rd we consider it to be a major-type scale, so we previously learned how to fit it around the major pentatonic scale.

However, now we're going to "break the rules" and combine it with the *minor* pentatonic scale.

Now, I know you're probably thinking, "Hang on a minute mate, you can't just start messing around with the laws of time, space and music" but you'd be wrong. Very wrong. Apart from the bit about time and space. I have no control over those things.

But when it comes to music, you'd be surprised about how much flexibility we have. In fact, a huge part of rock, blues, funk, country, pop and jazz vocabulary is created using this interplay between minor and major. More specifically, playing a minor 3rd (b3) in the melody and bending it slightly upwards towards major 3rd territory.

Let's look at how this works with minimal theory and maximum cool licks.

When you look at a diagram of Mixolydian notes superimposed onto the minor pentatonic scale, it does in fairness appear to be a bit of a mess.

The left-hand diagram shows the minor pentatonic scale in black with Mixolydian notes in white.

The middle diagram is a reminder of the major pentatonic notes you learned in the previous chapter. Again, these are shown in black with the Mixolydian notes in white.

The right-hand diagram shows the "pure" Mixolydian scale for reference.

Focus on the black pentatonic dots in the first two diagrams and you'll start to notice that when you combine the major and minor pentatonic scales you create a full Mixolydian scale, plus a cool, exciting b3. You can see it most clearly on the third and the first strings, although it exists on the bottom string too.

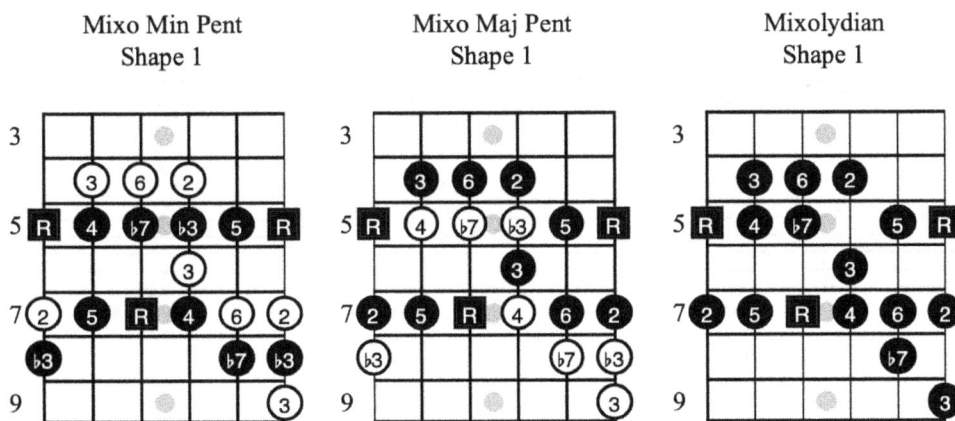

Mixo Min Pent Shape 1   Mixo Maj Pent Shape 1   Mixolydian Shape 1

Interestingly, you could also see this combination as a Dorian scale with a major 3rd. This shows you how closely the Mixolydian and Dorian scales are linked.

There was a lot of conceptual information there and you might be wondering what on earth we're going to do with it.

Let's start by focusing on how to use the b3.

The first thing to know is that you can play A Minor Pentatonic licks all day over an A7 groove, and you've probably already done this if you've played any blues guitar soloing. To make it work and sound bluesy, you will have found that you need to bend the b3 very slightly upwards (or indeed *all* the way upwards) towards the major 3rd to make it sound cool. This technique is called a *curl*. To demonstrate this, here are three simple minor pentatonic licks played over an A7 groove that use curls to push the b3 slightly up towards the major 3rd.

As the b3 (C) isn't in the A7 chord (A C# E G), bending it slightly sharp pushes it towards C# territory and that's why it sounds great.

You will see these curls happen on the 5th fret of the third string, and the 8th fret of the first string. Refer to the previous diagrams to reinforce your understanding of these locations.

Example 7a:

Example 7b:

Example 7c:

Now you've learned some simple pentatonic language, let's look at how we can use interplay between the major and minor pentatonic scales to create a flowing musical approach to playing Mixolydian ideas.

We will begin by exploring some of the movements between minor pentatonic and Mixolydian.

Scale Notes	A	B	C	C#	D	E	F	G
Minor Pentatonic	1		b3		4	5		b7
Mixolydian Mode	1	2		3	4	5	6	b7

We've already seen how the b3 to 3 movement works, so let's ignore that for the moment and we see that we can create a Mixolydian sound by adding the 2nd (9th) and 6th (13th) to the minor pentatonic scale. Does that ring any bells? It should do, because you covered those exact movements in Chapter Two – they are the same intervals as Dorian! That's great news as you've already done all the work for this chapter.

To create a Mixolydian sound using the minor pentatonic scale, you can simply think of adding those Dorian notes plus the bluesy movement from the b3 to the 3.

Let's dive straight in with some simple language that moves from minor pentatonic to Mixolydian using this approach. You'll see me use the 9th, 13th and the minor to major 3rd movement. However, I don't always use curls. I can hammer on or simply pick from the 5th to the 6th fret of the third string too.

Here are four licks to get you going. Throughout I'm "thinking" minor pentatonic phrasing then adding Mixolydian intervals as part of my phrase.

Example 7d:

Example 7e:

Example 7f:

Example 7g:

As we saw earlier, another way to think of Mixolydian is as a combination of minor and major pentatonic scales. In the next four examples I adjust my thinking slightly to incorporate this idea.

Now, instead of "thinking" minor pentatonic with added Mixolydian intervals, I focus on transitioning from minor pentatonic to major pentatonic (all the while adding the minor to major 3rd movement). Even though I play exactly the same bundle of notes as in the previous four examples, you'll hear that the effect is subtly different.

Here are four licks that take this approach.

Example 7h:

Example 7i:

Example 7j:

Example 7k:

Finally, let's reverse that approach. Instead of thinking minor to major pentatonic, I'm going to begin with major pentatonic ideas and transition into more minor pentatonic territory. Even when playing minor pentatonic ideas, I'll still add the occasional Mixolydian note, but you'll hear once again that this approach creates a subtly different effect.

Example 7l:

Example 7m:

Example 7n:

Example 7o:

In this chapter you've learned some musical way to approach Mixolydian soloing that use creative interplay between major and minor pentatonic scales. The sound of Mixolydian really leans into the kind of pentatonic phrasing we've explored, as it is at the heart of Texas blues and country. More often than not you'll find that Mixolydian is combined with minor pentatonic to create these types of phrases, whether it's the subtle b3 to 3 curl of the blues, or the more overt b3 to 3 hammer-on of country.

To recap:

We learned that the combination of the major and minor pentatonic scales gives us the notes of Mixolydian with an extra minor 3rd.

It is extremely common for guitarists to bend the minor 3rd up towards major 3rd territory and this is a very important sound in blues/rock guitar soloing.

Four common approaches to playing Mixolydian are:

1) Think minor pentatonic and add the 9th and 13th intervals from Mixolydian

2) Think minor pentatonic and transition into major pentatonic ideas

3) Think major pentatonic and transition into minor pentatonic ideas

4) Think major pentatonic and add the b7 and 11th intervals from Mixolydian (from Chapter Six)

Each of these approaches can create subtly different sounds as you favour different types of vocabulary. The best thing you can do is improvise for a few hours over the A7 backing track and see which approach yields the best results for you. This will change over the course of your playing career so never stop exploring!

Practice over different backing tracks and explore upbeat rock, blues and country to hear Mixolydian in action. The secret is to think of it not so much as a single scale, but as a combination of pentatonics.

Let's finish off with a few more shape one Mixolydian ideas that are slightly more advanced. Look out for the bends and expressive techniques I use to make these lines come to life.

There are some very important bends to take note of:

From b7 to Root

From 2 to b3

From b3 to 3

From 7 to b7

Keep an eye out for all of them, and the mini curl bend that just pushes the minor 3rd slightly towards major 3rd territory. There are about five or six different nuanced pitches between b3 and 3 if you're careful!

Example 7p:

Example 7q:

Example 7r:

Example 7s:

Chapter Eight: Mixolydian Shape Four

The previous two chapters covered the main ideas behind our Mixolydian soloing approach, and in this chapter I want to show you how to transfer them into shape four of the scale. Again, we will be working in the key of A.

Let's begin by comparing the shape four scale pattern of A Mixolydian with the corresponding A Major and A Minor Pentatonic scales. Notice that the root note is on the fifth string.

The left-hand diagram shows the minor pentatonic scale in black with Mixolydian notes in white.

The middle diagram shows the major pentatonic notes. Again, these are shown in black with the Mixolydian and notes in white.

The right-hand diagram shows the "pure" Mixolydian scale for reference.

Mixo Min Pent Shape 4   Mixo Maj Pent Shape 4   Mixolydian Shape 4

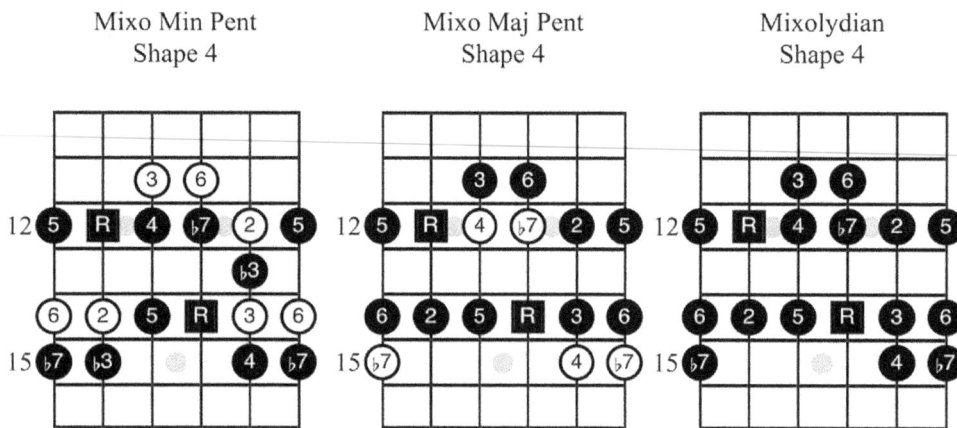

Once again, looking at Mixolydian notes superimposed onto the minor pentatonic scale seems like a bit of a mess. However, if you take a minute to look at each shape in turn you will start to see some patterns emerge.

Focus on the black pentatonic dots in the first two diagrams and you'll again see that by combining the notes of the major and minor pentatonic scales we create a full Mixolydian scale with the additional bluesy b3.

Let's learn this concept in shape four by learning some cool vocab. Remember our four approaches?

1) Think major pentatonic and add the b7 and 11th intervals from Mixolydian

2) Think minor pentatonic (using blues curls) and add the 9th and 13th intervals from Mixolydian

3) Think minor pentatonic and transition into major pentatonic ideas

4) Think major pentatonic and transition into minor pentatonic ideas

Each of these approaches can create subtly different sounds, as each one favours a different type of vocabulary.

Let's begin with a fairly "pure" A Mixolydian sound. Here are five licks based around A Major Pentatonic ideas that add the b7 and 11th intervals. Notice that I use bends, legato and other techniques to make these licks come alive. If you like the sound of a movement, explore it and write your own lines using it while jamming over the backing track.

Example 8a:

Example 8b:

Example 8c:

Example 8d:

Example 8e:

Now let's move on and learn some lines that are minor pentatonic based and add the 9th and 13th intervals from Mixolydian. Watch out for the bluesy curls that occur frequently throughout the licks. Once again, I make full use of bends and other expressive techniques to make the lines more vocal and musical. Isolate these ideas and explore them to create your own licks.

Example 8f:

Example 8g:

Example 8h:

Example 8i:

Example 8j:

The next lines take a similar approach but this time I'm "thinking" minor pentatonic then transitioning into the major pentatonic scale to access the remaining Mixolydian intervals. Remember, Major Pentatonic + Minor Pentatonic = Mixolydian + a b3!

Example 8k:

Example 8l:

Example 8m:

Example 8n:

Example 8o:

Finally, these ideas begin with the major pentatonic scale then transition into the minor pentatonic scale to give the lines a slightly more bluesy edge. Remember, combining major and minor pentatonic scales gives us all the intervals of Mixolydian plus that bluesy minor 3rd.

Example 8p:

Example 8q:

Example 8r:

Example 8s:

Example 8t:

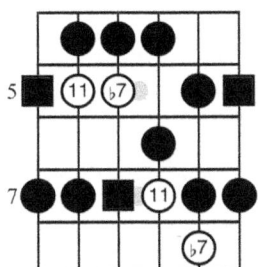

Example 8u:

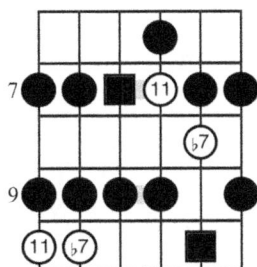

In this chapter I've not dwelled on any theory or process – you've covered enough of that by now to understand how to explore each approach to playing the Mixolydian mode in shape four. Instead, I've just given you a lot of vocabulary that is created by thinking differently about how we approach the Mixolydian sound.

The important thing is to get these phrases into your ears and explore what you can do by improvising around these sounds. Again, listen to upbeat rock, country and blues and you'll quickly start to recognise these ideas in action. Steal the ones you like and use them to create your own personal vocabulary.

Mixolydian is one of the most fun sounds to explore in rock guitar, so put on that A7 backing track and see how creative you can get!

When you're ready, apply the teaching in these chapters to all five shapes of the Mixolydian scale.

A Mixolydian Shape 1

A Mixolydian Shape 2

A Mixolydian Shape 3

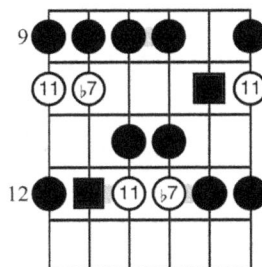

A Mixolydian
Shape 4

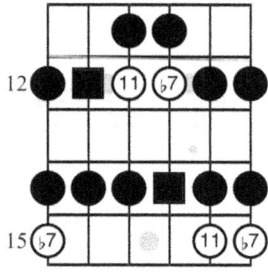

A Mixolydian
Shape 5

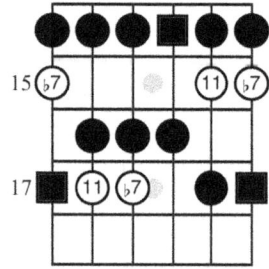

Chapter Nine: From Major Pentatonic to Major

The final scale we will look at in this book is the humble major scale. While it's been the building block of Western music for around 800 years, it is slightly less useful for guitarists as so much sound has been based around rock and blues since the invention of the electric guitar in the '50s.

When you consider the types of music that were emerging during that time period, and how the guitar's role shaped their development, it's no wonder that the language of modern guitar is based more around pentatonic scales, along with Dorian and Mixolydian.

Also, there are two notes in the major scale that can sound a bit clunky when played over more rocky backing tracks, these are the 4th and natural 7th. Now you may be thinking, "Hang on, that 4th sounded great in minor pentatonic and Mixolydian", and you'd be quite right, however both those scales have a b7, not a natural 7th like the major scale. There's something about the tritone (b5 interval) formed between the 4th and natural 7th that is a bit dissonant in rock and blues. You'll start to hear this as we play through the exercises. It is the 7th in particular that needs careful attention.

That aside, the Major scale is so important that you should know it fluently, and you will come across it in many types of music that aren't blues based.

Let's look at the first shape of the A Major scale and see how it fits around A Major Pentatonic.

Scale Notes	A	B	C#	D	E	F	G#
Major Pentatonic	1	2	3		5	6	
Major Scale	1	2	3	4 (11)	5	6	7

As you can see, the major scale can be thought of as a major pentatonic scale plus the 7th and 11th. I mentioned this earlier but it's always a good thing to repeat: the major scale is *identical* to the Mixolydian mode except for the 7th. Mixolydian has a b7 and Major has a natural 7th, so you've done a lot of the work here already.

A Major
Shape 1

A Mixolydian
Shape 1

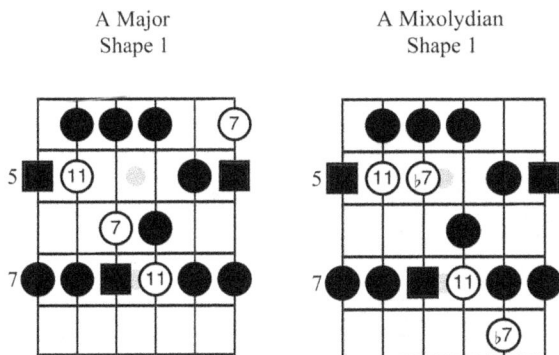

Play up and down the A Major Pentatonic scale, then play through again adding the A Major scale intervals

Example 9a:

Let's get started by exploring the transition from major pentatonic into the natural 7th of Major. Notice that it lives a semitone below the root note. We will begin by ascending the major pentatonic scale from the 9th and letting the 7th on the top string ring out. You'll here there's a slight tension between it and the backing track.

A Major Pentatonic
Shape 1

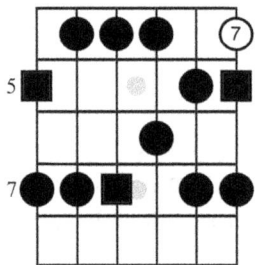

Example 9b:

This time I'll ascend from the 3rd on the third string up past the 7th, then descend back to it from above. Once again, you'll hear that slight tension.

Example 9c:

OK, cool. We know where the 7th is but it's sounding a bit sketchy. Let's deal with that now by playing an idea similar to Example 9b, but this time bending that 7th up a half-step to the root before resolving the idea.

Example 9d:

Now let's apply that bend to an idea similar to Example 9c.

Example 9e:

In the previous two examples you'll have heard how a simple half-step bend solves the tension that occurs by pausing on the 7th over a major chord. Remember though, it's unlikely that you'll be playing the major scale over a single chord and a more lifelike situation is playing it over a sequence that changes chord every one or two bars.

So, even if you find the 7th not to your taste in this context, it does sound great over loads of chords in a major chord progression.

For example, in the key of A, the 7th is G#, which is a great note to land on over pretty much any other chord in the key:

It's the 6th of B Minor, it's the 5th of C# Minor, it's the 3rd of E Major, it's the 9th of F# minor etc... all lovely colourful notes to target.

There are plenty of places in a major chord sequence where you can land on the 7th and it'll sound great, so don't think you have to avoid it, you just need to learn to listen to your playing and trust your ears.

With that in mind, let's use a backing track built from chords in the key of A Major and look again at how we can target that 7th interval. Begin by repeating the previous two examples then move onto the following ideas.

This first phrase ascends the major pentatonic then bends the 6th of scale (second string, 7th fret) up a tone to land on the 7th.

Example 9f:

The next phrase *targets* the 7th, so it is played just as the chord in the backing track changes to E Major. I land on it here, but you could once again bend up from the 6th.

Example 9g:

Here are a couple more ideas that use major pentatonic to target the higher 7th in this shape.

Example 9h:

Example 9i:

You might find that the other 7th in this shape is a bit too low pitched to be much use, but it's actually very common to target this as the backing track changes from A Major to E Major, as it really articulates the chord change. It is located on the fourth string 6th fret.

A Major Pentatonic
Shape 1

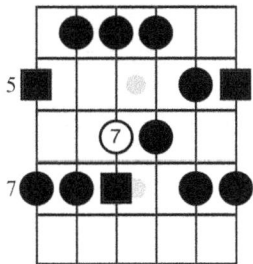

Let's begin with a simple idea that descends to this 7th.

Example 9j:

This phrase ascends through the A Major pentatonic scale and lands on the 7th.

Example 9k:

Finally, here are two slightly more musical ideas to target the 7th.

Example 9l:

Example 9m:

As always, spend time finding your own major pentatonic routes that are adapted to incorporate the 7th.

Example 9n:

We've covered finding the 4th/11th for every scale in this book, so I won't dwell on it here. Instead, here are four major pentatonic licks that include that note.

The following four licks are played over the major chord sequence and are built from the A Major Pentatonic scale + the 4th/11th. These (as you should know by now!) are located on the third string 7th fret and fifth string 5th fret.

A Major Pentatonic
Shape 1

A Major Pentatonic
Shape 1

You'll definitely see similarities between these and the major pentatonic + 4th lines in the Mixolydian chapters, as they include the same notes, however these will sound different because over the major backing track, my ears take the melodies to new places.

Example 9o:

Example 9p:

Example 9q:

Example 9r:

Finally, these four licks are built around the A Major Pentatonic scale and incorporate both the 7th and the 11th to include every note of the Major scale. As always, remember that the whole point of this exercise is to teach you to *think* of pentatonic phrasing, then add the other two scale notes as an additional flavour.

A Major
Shape 1

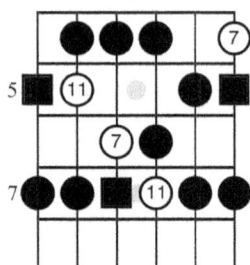

Example 9s:

```
A
e|--------------------------------------------|---------------------------|
B|--------------------5----------5------5------|--4--------5------4----5---|
G|---------4-----6---------6----7--------------|-------7-------------------|
D|----7---------------------------------------|--------------------------|
A|--------------------------------------------|---------------------------|
E|--------------------------------------------|---------------------------|
```

Example 9t:

```
A
e|--------------------------------------------|---------------------------|
B|--------------------------------------------|---------------------------|
G|--------------------4-----6----4----7-------|-------------4----6----7---|
D|---4-----7----5-----------7-----------------|--6----7------------------|
A|--------------------------------------------|---------------------------|
E|--------------------------------------------|---------------------------|
```

Example 9u:

```
A
e|--------------------------------------------|---------------------------|
B|---5-----7----5-----7----6----4-------------|-----------------4----7---|
G|-----------------------------------7----6---|--4----6----7-------------|
D|--------------------------------------------|---------------------------|
A|--------------------------------------------|---------------------------|
E|--------------------------------------------|---------------------------|
```

Example 9v:

```
A
e|--------------------------------------------|---------------------5----|
B|--------------------------------------------|----------4----6----5-----|
G|--------------------------------4----7------|--6-----------------------|
D|---5----4----7----5----4----7---------------|--------------------------|
A|---5----------------------------------------|--------------------------|
E|--------------------------------------------|--------------------------|
```

When you've memorized all the licks in this chapter, spend some time jamming over the backing track and creating your own lines using the pentatonic + intervals approach.

Chapter Ten: Major Continued

Let's round off the book by looking at the A Major scale shape four up at the 12th fret. As always, compare the major pentatonic scale to the Major scale and look to see where the extra notes live. You learned this major pentatonic scale shape in Chapter Eight.

Remember, the Major scale is formed from the major pentatonic scale + a 7th and an 11th. Notice that the highest 7th is very slightly out of position, but this is still a common shape.

We did most of the hard work in the previous chapters, so let's cut straight to the chase. The most useful 7ths are located on the first string 14th fret, and the third string 13th fret.

A Major
Shape 4

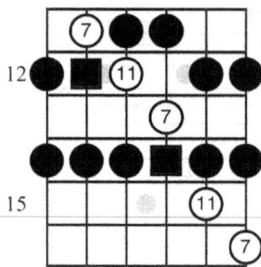

The first two ideas use the major pentatonic shape to target the higher 7th.

A Major Pentatonic
Shape 4

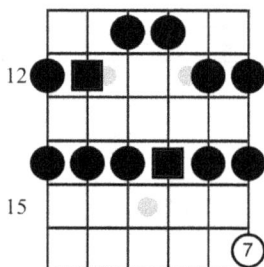

Example 10a:

Example 10b:

The next two phrases turn the previous two approaches into more melodic phrases using bends and musical techniques.

Example 10c:

The next four ideas repeat the previous approach but use the major pentatonic scale to target the 7th on the third string, 13th fret. There are two simple targeting ideas followed by two more melodic phrases.

A Major Pentatonic
Shape 4

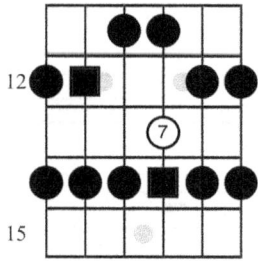

Example 10d:

Example 10e:

Example 10f:

102

Example 10g:

These four phrases repeat the process and use the major pentatonic scale to target the 11th on the second string, 15th fret.

A Major Pentatonic
Shape 4

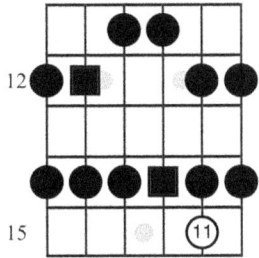

Example 10h:

Example 10i:

Example 10j:

Example 10k:

Now we'll do the same thing but use the major pentatonic scale to target the 11th located on the fourth string 12th fret.

A Major Pentatonic
Shape 4

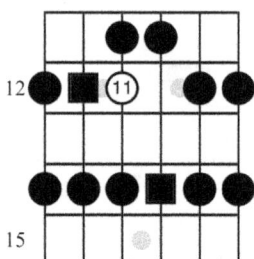

Example 10l:

Example 10m:

Example 10n:

Example 10o:

Next, let's learn some more lick-based vocabulary built from the major pentatonic + 4ths approach. These four licks contain some fun ideas.

Example 10p:

Example 10q:

Example 10r:

Example 10s:

Finally, here are four licks that take a major pentatonic approach and add the 11ths and 7ths to include every note of the A Major scale. Remember, I *think* pentatonic to access that natural phrasing, then add the other intervals to colour my sound. These intervals sound very different over each chord in the backing track sequence, so try playing these phrases at different points in the bar so you can hear their effect on the music. Something that might sound challenging in one place in the sequence will sound great in another.

As always, trust your ears and be prepared to explore!

Example 10t:

Example 10u:

Example 10v:

Example 10w:

Finally, here are all five shapes of the Major scale so that you can continue your explorations.

Conclusion

We've covered a huge amount of ground in this book and I hope you have learned a lot. The concept of taking a humble pentatonic scale and adding a couple of notes to introduce a whole new bunch of colours should feel like a simple idea to you now, but it's amazing the number of people who think that soloing with modes must require a completely different approach to soloing with pentatonics.

In fact, you could see this aspect of soloing in three different ways:

1) Soloing with only pentatonic/blues scale ideas

2) Soloing with pentatonic ideas that add modal intervals

3) Soloing with purely modal ideas.

All three of these approaches have a different place and sound. I'm not one to generalise, but if I had to, I'd suggest that:

1) Exclusively pentatonic/blues scale ideas would be appropriate when playing in an early blues style.

2) Pentatonic + introducing some modal intervals would be evocative of '60s to late '70s rock

3) Exclusively modal scale soloing (with very few pentatonic phrases) would be more akin to the "big hair" guitar virtuoso players of the '80s and '90s.

Now, please don't come at me on social media for saying that, because I am 100% generalising here and *of course* Paul Gilbert plays a lot of tasty bluesy ideas, etc… this is just to give you a starting point for your listening adventures.

A great player to listen to for the crossing over of pentatonic blues ideas with the odd modal interval is actually Jimi Hendrix and a lot of blues-rock guitarists of the '60s and '70s, like Clapton (particularly in Cream), Stevie Ray Vaughan and Rory Gallagher.

Also check out a lot of "classic rock" players like Riche Blackmore Jimi Page, Dave Gilmour, Mark Knopfler and Brian May.

Again, I stress that I'm wildly generalising here, so please let's keep the angry emails to a minimum ;-)

Finally, there are a few modes we've not covered here that you'll probably want to check out on your travels. We've ignored Locrian because it's a bit of a weird one and not used very much, but aside from that, the two modes we've not covered are Lydian and Phrygian.

Lydian is a major mode with the spelling 1 2 3 #4 5 6 7 and can be thought of as a major pentatonic scale with an added #4 (#11) and 7.

Shapes one and four of Lydian are shown below to get you started.

A Lydian
Shape 1

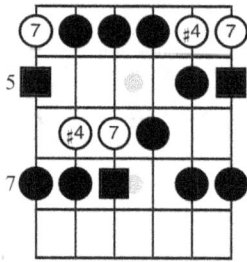

A Lydian
Shape 4

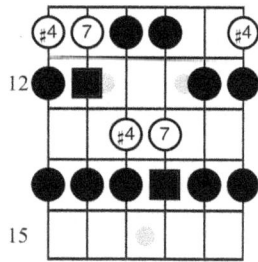

Phrygian is a minor mode with the spelling 1 b2 b3 4 5 b6 b7 and can be thought of as a minor pentatonic scale with an added b2 (b9) and a b6 (b13)

Shapes one and four of Phrygian are shown below to get you started.

A Phrygian
Shape 1

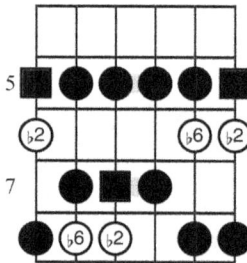

A Phrygian
Shape 4

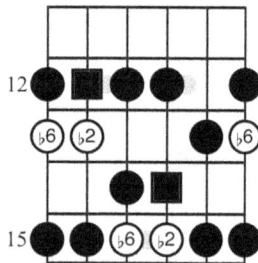

Explore these scales in the same way as you have done for all the others in this book and enjoy your musical journey!

Have fun,

Joseph

www.ingramcontent.com/pod-product-compliance
Lightning Source LLC
Chambersburg PA
CBHW081132090426
42737CB00018B/3315